Happy Travels!

Today's Date:

_____

What I did, things I saw, people I met...

- _____

- _____

- _____

- _____

- _____

My favorite part of today:

_____

_____

_____

What I will do tomorrow:

_____

_____

_____

Explore . Enjoy . Rest . Repeat

Draw today's adventures!

Stick your envelope, postcard, stickers or keepsakes, right here ↓

Today's Date:

_____

What I did, things I saw, people I met...

- _____
- _____
- _____
- _____
- _____

My favorite part of today:

_____

_____

_____

What I will do tomorrow:

_____

_____

_____

Explore . Enjoy . Rest . Repeat

Draw today's adventures!

Stick your envelope, postcard, stickers or keepsakes, right here ↓

Today's Date:

_____

What I did, things I saw, people I met...

- _____
- _____
- _____
- _____
- _____

My favorite part of today:

_____

_____

_____

What I will do tomorrow:

_____

_____

_____

Draw today's adventures!

Stick your envelope, postcard, stickers or keepsakes, right here ↓

Today's Date:

_____

What I did, things I saw, people I met...

- _____

- _____

- _____

- _____

- _____

My favorite part of today:

_____

_____

_____

What I will do tomorrow:

_____

_____

_____

Explore . Enjoy . Rest . Repeat

Draw today's adventures!

Stick your envelope, postcard, stickers or keepsakes, right here ⬇

Today's Date:

_____

What I did, things I saw, people I met...

- _____
- _____
- _____
- _____
- _____

My favorite part of today:

_____

_____

_____

What I will do tomorrow:

_____

_____

_____

Explore . Enjoy . Rest . Repeat

Draw today's adventures!

Stick your envelope, postcard, stickers or keepsakes, right here ↓

Today's Date:

_____

What I did, things I saw, people I met...

- _____

- _____

- _____

- _____

- _____

My favorite part of today:

_____

_____

_____

What I will do tomorrow:

_____

_____

_____

Explore . Enjoy . Rest . Repeat

Draw today's adventures!

Stick your envelope, postcard, stickers or keepsakes, right here ⬇

Today's Date:

_____

What I did, things I saw, people I met...

- _____

- _____

- _____

- _____

- _____

My favorite part of today:

_____

_____

_____

What I will do tomorrow:

_____

_____

_____

Draw today's adventures!

Stick your envelope, postcard, stickers or keepsakes, right here ↓

Today's Date:

_____

What I did, things I saw, people I met...

- _____
- _____
- _____
- _____
- _____

My favorite part of today:

_____

_____

_____

What I will do tomorrow:

_____

_____

_____

Explore . Enjoy . Rest . Repeat

Draw today's adventures!

Stick your envelope, postcard, stickers or keepsakes, right here ⬇

Today's Date:

_____

What I did, things I saw, people I met...

- _____

- _____

- _____

- _____

- _____

My favorite part of today:

_____

_____

_____

What I will do tomorrow:

_____

_____

_____

Draw today's adventures!

Stick your envelope, postcard, stickers or keepsakes, right here ⬇

Explore . Enjoy . Rest . Repeat

Today's Date:

_____

What I did, things I saw, people I met...

- _____
- _____
- _____
- _____
- _____

My favorite part of today:

_____

_____

_____

What I will do tomorrow:

_____

_____

_____

Draw today's adventures!

Stick your envelope, postcard, stickers or keepsakes, right here ⬇

Today's Date:

_____

What I did, things I saw, people I met...

- _____
- _____
- _____
- _____
- _____

My favorite part of today:

_____

_____

_____

What I will do tomorrow:

_____

_____

_____

Explore . Enjoy . Rest . Repeat

Draw today's adventures!

Stick your envelope, postcard, stickers or keepsakes, right here ↓

Today's Date:

_____

What I did, things I saw, people I met...

- _____
- _____
- _____
- _____
- _____

My favorite part of today:

_____

_____

_____

What I will do tomorrow:

_____

_____

_____

Draw today's adventures!

Stick your envelope, postcard, stickers or keepsakes, right here ⬇

Today's Date:

_____

What I did, things I saw, people I met...

- _____

- _____

- _____

- _____

- _____

My favorite part of today:

_____

_____

_____

What I will do tomorrow:

_____

_____

_____

Draw today's adventures!

Stick your envelope, postcard, stickers or keepsakes, right here ⬇

Today's Date:

_____

What I did, things I saw, people I met...

- _____
- _____
- _____
- _____
- _____

My favorite part of today:

_____

_____

_____

What I will do tomorrow:

_____

_____

_____

Explore . Enjoy . Rest . Repeat

Draw today's adventures!

Stick your envelope, postcard, stickers or keepsakes, right here ↓

Today's Date:

_____

What I did, things I saw, people I met...

- _____

- _____

- _____

- _____

- _____

My favorite part of today:

_____

_____

_____

What I will do tomorrow:

_____

_____

_____

Explore . Enjoy . Rest . Repeat

Draw today's adventures!

Stick your envelope, postcard, stickers or keepsakes, right here ⬇

Today's Date:

_____

What I did, things I saw, people I met...

- _____
- _____
- _____
- _____
- _____

My favorite part of today:

_____

_____

_____

What I will do tomorrow:

_____

_____

_____

Draw today's adventures!

Stick your envelope, postcard, stickers or keepsakes, right here ↓

Today's Date:

_____

What I did, things I saw, people I met...

- _____
- _____
- _____
- _____
- _____

My favorite part of today:

_____

_____

_____

What I will do tomorrow:

_____

_____

_____

Explore . Enjoy . Rest . Repeat

Draw today's adventures!

Stick your envelope, postcard, stickers or keepsakes, right here ↓

Today's Date:

_____

What I did, things I saw, people I met...

- _____
- _____
- _____
- _____
- _____

My favorite part of today:

_____

_____

_____

What I will do tomorrow:

_____

_____

_____

Draw today's adventures!

Stick your envelope, postcard, stickers or keepsakes, right here ⬇

Today's Date:

_____

What I did, things I saw, people I met...

- _____
- _____
- _____
- _____
- _____

My favorite part of today:

_____

_____

_____

What I will do tomorrow:

_____

_____

_____

Explore . Enjoy . Rest . Repeat

Draw today's adventures!

Stick your envelope, postcard, stickers or keepsakes, right here ⬇

Today's Date:

_____

What I did, things I saw, people I met...

- _____

- _____

- _____

- _____

- _____

My favorite part of today:

_____

_____

_____

What I will do tomorrow:

_____

_____

_____

Draw today's adventures!

Stick your envelope, postcard, stickers or keepsakes, right here ⬇

Today's Date:

_____

What I did, things I saw, people I met...

- _____

- _____

- _____

- _____

- _____

My favorite part of today:

_____

_____

_____

What I will do tomorrow:

_____

_____

_____

Draw today's adventures!

Stick your envelope, postcard, stickers or keepsakes, right here ⬇

Today's Date:

_____

What I did, things I saw, people I met...

- _____
- _____
- _____
- _____
- _____

My favorite part of today:

_____

_____

_____

What I will do tomorrow:

_____

_____

_____

Draw today's adventures!

Stick your envelope, postcard, stickers or keepsakes, right here ↓

Today's Date:

_____

What I did, things I saw, people I met...

- _____
- _____
- _____
- _____
- _____

My favorite part of today:

_____

_____

_____

What I will do tomorrow:

_____

_____

_____

Explore . Enjoy . Rest . Repeat

Draw today's adventures!

Stick your envelope, postcard, stickers or keepsakes, right here ↓

Today's Date:

_____

What I did, things I saw, people I met...

- _____
- _____
- _____
- _____
- _____

My favorite part of today:

_____

_____

_____

What I will do tomorrow:

_____

_____

_____

Explore . Enjoy . Rest . Repeat

Draw today's adventures!

Stick your envelope, postcard, stickers or keepsakes, right here ↓

Today's Date:

_____

What I did, things I saw, people I met...

- _____

- _____

- _____

- _____

- _____

My favorite part of today:

_____

_____

_____

What I will do tomorrow:

_____

_____

_____

Explore . Enjoy . Rest . Repeat

Draw today's adventures!

Stick your envelope, postcard, stickers or keepsakes, right here ⬇

Today's Date:

_____

What I did, things I saw, people I met...

- _____
- _____
- _____
- _____
- _____

My favorite part of today:

_____

_____

_____

What I will do tomorrow:

_____

_____

_____

Draw today's adventures!

Stick your envelope, postcard, stickers or keepsakes, right here ↓

Today's Date:

_____

What I did, things I saw, people I met...

- _____

- _____

- _____

- _____

- _____

My favorite part of today:

_____

_____

_____

What I will do tomorrow:

_____

_____

_____

Draw today's adventures!

Stick your envelope, postcard, stickers or keepsakes, right here ⬇

Today's Date:

_____

What I did, things I saw, people I met...

- _____
- _____
- _____
- _____
- _____

My favorite part of today:

_____

_____

_____

What I will do tomorrow:

_____

_____

_____

Explore . Enjoy . Rest . Repeat

Draw today's adventures!

Stick your envelope, postcard, stickers or keepsakes, right here ↓

Today's Date:

_____

What I did, things I saw, people I met...

- _____

- _____

- _____

- _____

- _____

My favorite part of today:

_____

_____

_____

What I will do tomorrow:

_____

_____

_____

Draw today's adventures!

Stick your envelope, postcard, stickers or keepsakes, right here ↓

Today's Date:

_____

What I did, things I saw, people I met...

- _____

- _____

- _____

- _____

- _____

My favorite part of today:

_____

_____

_____

What I will do tomorrow:

_____

_____

_____

Draw today's adventures!

Stick your envelope, postcard, stickers or keepsakes, right here ⬇

Today's Date:

_____

What I did, things I saw, people I met...

- _____

- _____

- _____

- _____

- _____

My favorite part of today:

_____

_____

_____

What I will do tomorrow:

_____

_____

_____

Draw today's adventures!

Stick your envelope, postcard, stickers or keepsakes, right here ↓

Explore . Enjoy . Rest . Repeat

Today's Date:

_____

What I did, things I saw, people I met...

- _____

- _____

- _____

- _____

- _____

My favorite part of today:

_____

_____

_____

What I will do tomorrow:

_____

_____

_____

Draw today's adventures!

Stick your envelope, postcard, stickers or keepsakes, right here ↓

Explore . Enjoy . Rest . Repeat

Today's Date:

_____

What I did, things I saw, people I met...

- _____
- _____
- _____
- _____
- _____

My favorite part of today:

_____

_____

_____

What I will do tomorrow:

_____

_____

_____

Draw today's adventures!

Stick your envelope, postcard, stickers or keepsakes, right here ⬇

Today's Date:

_____

What I did, things I saw, people I met...

- _____

- _____

- _____

- _____

- _____

My favorite part of today:

_____

_____

_____

What I will do tomorrow:

_____

_____

_____

Draw today's adventures!

Stick your envelope, postcard, stickers or keepsakes, right here ⬇

Today's Date:

_____

What I did, things I saw, people I met...

- _____

- _____

- _____

- _____

- _____

My favorite part of today:

_____

_____

_____

What I will do tomorrow:

_____

_____

_____

Draw today's adventures!

Stick your envelope, postcard, stickers or keepsakes, right here ⬇

Today's Date:

_____

What I did, things I saw, people I met...

- _____

- _____

- _____

- _____

- _____

My favorite part of today:

_____

_____

_____

What I will do tomorrow:

_____

_____

_____

Draw today's adventures!

Stick your envelope, postcard, stickers or keepsakes, right here ⬇

Today's Date:

_____

What I did, things I saw, people I met...

- _____
- _____
- _____
- _____
- _____

My favorite part of today:

_____

_____

_____

What I will do tomorrow:

_____

_____

_____

Explore . Enjoy . Rest . Repeat

Draw today's adventures!

Stick your envelope, postcard, stickers or keepsakes, right here ⬇

Today's Date:

_____

What I did, things I saw, people I met...

- _____

- _____

- _____

- _____

- _____

My favorite part of today:

_____

_____

_____

What I will do tomorrow:

_____

_____

_____

Draw today's adventures!

Stick your envelope, postcard, stickers or keepsakes, right here ⬇

Today's Date:

_____

What I did, things I saw, people I met...

- _____

- _____

- _____

- _____

- _____

My favorite part of today:

_____

_____

_____

What I will do tomorrow:

_____

_____

_____

Draw today's adventures!

Stick your envelope, postcard, stickers or keepsakes, right here ↓

Explore . Enjoy . Rest . Repeat

Today's Date:

_____

What I did, things I saw, people I met...

- _____
- _____
- _____
- _____
- _____

My favorite part of today:

_____

_____

_____

What I will do tomorrow:

_____

_____

_____

Draw today's adventures!

Stick your envelope, postcard, stickers or keepsakes, right here ⬇

Today's Date:

_____

What I did, things I saw, people I met...

- _____
- _____
- _____
- _____
- _____

My favorite part of today:

_____

_____

_____

What I will do tomorrow:

_____

_____

_____

Draw today's adventures!

Stick your envelope, postcard, stickers or keepsakes, right here ⬇

Explore . Enjoy . Rest . Repeat

Today's Date:

_____

What I did, things I saw, people I met...

- _____
- _____
- _____
- _____
- _____

My favorite part of today:

_____

_____

_____

What I will do tomorrow:

_____

_____

_____

Explore . Enjoy . Rest . Repeat

Draw today's adventures!

Stick your envelope, postcard, stickers or keepsakes, right here ⬇

Today's Date:

_____

What I did, things I saw, people I met...

- ● _____
- ● _____
- ● _____
- ● _____
- ● _____

My favorite part of today:

_____

_____

_____

What I will do tomorrow:

_____

_____

_____

Explore . Enjoy . Rest . Repeat

Draw today's adventures!

Stick your envelope, postcard, stickers or keepsakes, right here ⬇

Explore . Enjoy . Rest . Repeat

Today's Date:

_____

What I did, things I saw, people I met...

- _____
- _____
- _____
- _____
- _____

My favorite part of today:

_____

_____

_____

What I will do tomorrow:

_____

_____

_____

Draw today's adventures!

Stick your envelope, postcard, stickers or keepsakes, right here ⬇

Today's Date:

_____

What I did, things I saw, people I met...

- ● _____
- ● _____
- ● _____
- ● _____
- ● _____

My favorite part of today:

_____

_____

_____

What I will do tomorrow:

_____

_____

_____

Draw today's adventures!

Stick your envelope, postcard, stickers or keepsakes, right here ⬇

Today's Date:

_____

What I did, things I saw, people I met...

- • _____

- • _____

- • _____

- • _____

- • _____

My favorite part of today:

_____

_____

_____

What I will do tomorrow:

_____

_____

_____

Explore . Enjoy . Rest . Repeat

Draw today's adventures!

Stick your envelope, postcard, stickers or keepsakes, right here ⬇

Today's Date:

_____

What I did, things I saw, people I met...

- _____

- _____

- _____

- _____

- _____

My favorite part of today:

_____

_____

_____

What I will do tomorrow:

_____

_____

_____

Draw today's adventures!

Stick your envelope, postcard, stickers or keepsakes, right here ↓

Explore . Enjoy . Rest . Repeat

Today's Date:

_____

What I did, things I saw, people I met...

- _____

- _____

- _____

- _____

- _____

My favorite part of today:

_____

_____

_____

What I will do tomorrow:

_____

_____

_____

Draw today's adventures!

Stick your envelope, postcard, stickers or keepsakes, right here ⬇

Today's Date:

_____

What I did, things I saw, people I met...

- _____

- _____

- _____

- _____

- _____

My favorite part of today:

_____

_____

_____

What I will do tomorrow:

_____

_____

_____

Explore . Enjoy . Rest . Repeat

Draw today's adventures!

Stick your envelope, postcard, stickers or keepsakes, right here ↓